EMMANUEL JOSEPH

A Symphony of Flourishing, Aligning Health, Wealth, and Human Connections

Copyright © 2025 by Emmanuel Joseph

All rights reserved. No part of this publication may be reproduced, stored or transmitted in any form or by any means, electronic, mechanical, photocopying, recording, scanning, or otherwise without written permission from the publisher. It is illegal to copy this book, post it to a website, or distribute it by any other means without permission.

First edition

This book was professionally typeset on Reedsy.
Find out more at reedsy.com

Contents

1 Chapter 1   1

1

Chapter 1

Chapter 1: The Overture of Life Life, much like a symphony, is composed of various elements that harmonize to create a beautiful existence. At the heart of this symphony lies the delicate balance between health, wealth, and human connections. Understanding how these three pillars intertwine is essential for leading a fulfilling life. Health provides the foundation upon which we build our lives, wealth offers the resources to pursue our dreams, and human connections bring meaning and joy to our journey.

In our pursuit of health, we must recognize that it extends beyond the absence of illness. True health encompasses physical, mental, and emotional well-being. It's about nurturing our bodies through nutrition, exercise, and restful sleep. Mental health, often overlooked, plays a crucial role in our overall wellness. Managing stress, cultivating resilience, and seeking support when needed are vital components of a healthy life.

Wealth, on the other hand, is not merely a measure of financial success. It's about achieving a state of financial stability that allows us to live comfortably and pursue our passions. Building wealth requires prudent financial planning, wise investments, and a mindset of abundance. Wealth enables us to access better healthcare, education, and opportunities, ultimately enhancing our quality of life.

Human connections, the final piece of the symphony, are the relationships we forge with family, friends, and our community. These connections provide emotional support, a sense of belonging, and shared experiences that enrich our lives. Strong relationships are built on trust, empathy, and open communication. They require effort and time but offer immeasurable rewards in return. Aligning health, wealth, and human connections is the key to a flourishing life, and it begins with understanding their individual significance and interplay.

Chapter 2: The Harmony of Physical Health Physical health forms the cornerstone of a vibrant life. It's the energy that propels us forward and the resilience that helps us overcome challenges. To achieve optimal physical health, we must prioritize nutrition, exercise, and preventive care. Nutrition fuels our bodies, providing the essential vitamins, minerals, and nutrients needed for growth and repair. A balanced diet, rich in fruits, vegetables, lean proteins, and whole grains, is fundamental to maintaining good health.

Exercise, another crucial component, strengthens our muscles, improves cardiovascular health, and enhances mental clarity. Engaging in regular physical activity, whether it's a brisk walk, yoga, or strength training, has numerous benefits. It boosts our mood, reduces stress, and increases our longevity. Finding an exercise routine that we enjoy and can sustain is key to reaping these benefits.

Preventive care is the proactive approach to maintaining health. Regular check-ups, screenings, and vaccinations help identify and address potential health issues before they become serious. It's about being proactive rather than reactive, taking charge of our health, and making informed decisions. Additionally, adopting healthy habits such as staying hydrated, getting sufficient sleep, and avoiding harmful substances contributes to our overall well-being.

Incorporating these elements into our daily lives requires commitment and mindfulness. It's about making small, consistent changes that lead to significant improvements over time. By prioritizing our physical health, we lay a strong foundation for the other aspects of our lives to flourish. Physical health is not just a goal; it's a lifelong journey that evolves with us as we grow and change.

Chapter 3: The Melody of Mental Well-being Mental well-being is the serene melody that brings balance and peace to our lives. It's the mental fortitude that allows us to navigate the complexities of life with grace and resilience. Mental health is deeply interconnected with our physical health and overall quality of life. It's essential to recognize the importance of nurturing our minds just as we do our bodies.

One of the primary aspects of mental well-being is managing stress. Life's demands and pressures can lead to chronic stress, which negatively impacts our health. Effective stress management techniques such as mindfulness, meditation, and deep breathing exercises can help us stay grounded and centered. Creating a healthy work-life balance and setting boundaries are also crucial in reducing stress.

Resilience, the ability to bounce back from adversity, is another vital component of mental well-being. Building resilience involves cultivating a positive mindset, developing coping strategies, and seeking support when needed. It's about embracing challenges as opportunities for growth and learning. Resilience enables us to face life's ups and downs with a sense of inner strength and confidence.

Emotional intelligence, the ability to understand and manage our emotions, plays a significant role in our mental well-being. It involves self-awareness, empathy, and effective communication. By becoming more attuned to our emotions and those of others, we can navigate relationships and interactions with greater ease. Practicing gratitude, kindness, and self-compassion also contributes to our emotional well-being.

Mental health is not a destination but an ongoing journey. It's about making time for self-care, seeking professional help when needed, and continuously working on our mental well-being. By prioritizing our mental health, we create a harmonious balance that enhances our overall quality of life. A healthy mind is the foundation upon which we build a flourishing and fulfilling life.

Chapter 4: The Cadence of Financial Stability Financial stability is the steady cadence that underpins our sense of security and freedom. It's the assurance that we can meet our basic needs, pursue our goals, and handle unexpected expenses. Achieving financial stability requires careful planning, disciplined saving, and informed decision-making. It's about creating a solid financial foundation that supports our aspirations and dreams.

One of the first steps towards financial stability is budgeting. A well-crafted budget helps us track our income and expenses, ensuring that we live within our means. It's about making conscious choices and prioritizing our spending. By setting financial goals and creating a savings plan, we can build a safety net that provides peace of mind.

Investing wisely is another essential aspect of financial stability. Investments, whether in stocks, real estate, or education, can help grow our wealth over time. It's about understanding the risks and rewards and making informed decisions. Diversifying our investments and seeking professional advice can also contribute to our financial success.

Debt management is a crucial component of financial stability. High levels of debt can create stress and hinder our ability to save and invest. Developing a plan to pay off debt and avoid unnecessary borrowing is essential. It's about making responsible financial choices and maintaining a healthy credit score.

Financial education is the foundation of financial stability. Understanding basic financial concepts, such as interest rates, inflation, and retirement planning, empowers us to make informed decisions. Continuously educating ourselves and staying informed about financial trends and opportunities is key to long-term success. Financial stability is not just about accumulating wealth; it's about creating a balanced and secure financial life that allows us to thrive.

Chapter 5: The Resonance of Relationships Relationships are the resonant chords that add depth and richness to our lives. They provide emotional support, companionship, and a sense of belonging. Building and maintaining strong relationships requires effort, empathy, and effective communication. It's about nurturing connections that bring joy, comfort, and meaning to our lives.

Family relationships are the foundation of our social support system. They offer unconditional love, guidance, and a sense of identity. Strengthening family bonds involves spending quality time together, expressing appreciation, and resolving conflicts with compassion. It's about creating a supportive and nurturing environment where everyone feels valued.

Friendships, another vital aspect of our social life, bring joy, laughter, and shared experiences. Building lasting friendships requires mutual trust, respect, and genuine interest in each other's lives. It's about being there for each other through life's ups and downs and celebrating each other's successes. Friendships enrich our lives and contribute to our emotional well-being.

Community connections also play a significant role in our lives. Being part of a community provides a sense of belonging and shared purpose. Engaging in community activities, volunteering, and supporting local initiatives foster a sense of connection and fulfillment. It's about contributing to the greater good and building a network of support.

Romantic relationships, based on love and partnership, add an intimate dimension to our lives. Building a healthy romantic relationship requires trust, communication, and mutual respect. It's about understanding each other's needs, being supportive, and growing together as a couple. A strong romantic relationship enhances our overall well-being and happiness.

Relationships are the fabric of our social life, and nurturing them requires time, effort, and commitment. By prioritizing our relationships and investing in meaningful connections, we create a support system that enhances our quality of life. Healthy relationships are a cornerstone of a flourishing life.

Chapter 6: The Rhythm of Work-Life Balance Work-life balance is the steady rhythm that allows us to navigate the demands of work and personal life. It's about finding harmony between our professional responsibilities and personal well-being. Achieving work-life balance requires setting boundaries, prioritizing self-care, and making time for the things that matter most.

One of the key aspects of work-life balance is time management. Effective time management helps us allocate our time and energy to various tasks and responsibilities. It's about setting realistic goals, prioritizing tasks, and avoiding procrastination. By managing our time efficiently, we can reduce stress and create a more balanced life.

Setting boundaries is another crucial component of work-life balance. Boundaries help us establish limits and protect our personal time. It's about learning to say no, delegating tasks, and avoiding overcommitment. By setting clear boundaries, we can prevent burnout and create a healthier work environment.

Self-care is essential for maintaining work-life balance. Self-care involves taking time for ourselves and engaging in activities that rejuvenate and energize us. It's about prioritizing our physical, mental, and emotional well-being. Whether it's taking a walk, reading a book, or spending time with loved ones, self-care is a vital part of a balanced life.

Flexibility and adaptability are also important in achieving work-life balance. Life is unpredictable, and our priorities may shift from time to time. Being flexible and adaptable allows us to navigate these changes with ease. It's about being open to new opportunities and finding creative solutions on establishing harmony between work and personal life.

Another essential aspect of work-life balance is pursuing hobbies and interests. Engaging in activities we enjoy brings us joy and helps us recharge. It's about making time for creativity, relaxation, and fun. Hobbies can also provide a sense of accomplishment and fulfillment, contributing to our overall well-being.

Achieving work-life balance is an ongoing process that requires mindfulness and intentionality. It's about regularly assessing our priorities, setting goals, and making adjustments as needed. By creating a balanced life, we can enhance our productivity, well-being, and overall satisfaction.

Chapter 7: The Symphony of Emotional Intelligence Emotional intelligence is the harmonious symphony that enables us to understand and manage our emotions and those of others. It's the ability to navigate social interactions with empathy, self-awareness, and effective communication. Developing emotional intelligence enhances our relationships, decision-making, and overall quality of life.

Self-awareness is the foundation of emotional intelligence. It involves recognizing our emotions, strengths, and weaknesses. By being aware of our feelings and how they influence our behavior, we can make more conscious choices. Practicing mindfulness and reflection can help us develop greater self-awareness.

Empathy, the ability to understand and share the feelings of others, is another crucial component of emotional intelligence. Empathy allows us to connect with others on a deeper level and build strong relationships. It involves active listening, showing compassion, and validating others' emotions. Cultivating empathy enhances our social interactions and fosters a sense of connection and understanding.

Effective communication is essential for expressing our emotions and needs while understanding those of others. It involves active listening, clear expression, and non-verbal cues. By improving our communication skills, we can navigate conflicts, build trust, and strengthen our relationships. It's about being assertive while respecting others' perspectives.

Emotional regulation, the ability to manage our emotions, is also a vital aspect of emotional intelligence. It involves recognizing and addressing negative emotions constructively. Techniques such as deep breathing, journaling, and seeking support can help us regulate our emotions. Emotional regulation enhances our resilience and well-being.

Developing emotional intelligence is a lifelong journey that requires practice and dedication. By enhancing our emotional intelligence, we can create more meaningful connections, make better decisions, and lead a more fulfilling life.

Chapter 8: The Crescendo of Purpose Finding purpose is the crescendo that gives our lives direction and meaning. It's the driving force that motivates us to pursue our goals and aspirations. Discovering our purpose involves exploring our passions, values, and strengths. It's about aligning our actions with what truly matters to us.

One way to find purpose is by reflecting on our interests and passions. What activities bring us joy and fulfillment? What causes do we feel passionate about? By identifying our interests, we can explore ways to incorporate them into our lives. Pursuing our passions can lead to a greater sense of purpose and satisfaction.

Values play a significant role in shaping our purpose. Understanding our core values helps us make decisions that align with our principles. It's about reflecting on what is most important to us and prioritizing those values in our daily lives. Living in accordance with our values creates a sense of integrity and fulfillment.

Strengths are the unique qualities and talents that we possess. Recognizing and leveraging our strengths allows us to excel and make a positive impact. It's about focusing on what we do best and finding opportunities to use those strengths. Utilizing our strengths can enhance our sense of purpose and achievement.

Setting meaningful goals is another way to create purpose. Goals provide a sense of direction and motivation. It's about setting specific, achievable objectives that align with our passions, values, and strengths. Working towards these goals can bring a sense of accomplishment and purpose.

Finding purpose is an ongoing journey that evolves with us. It's about continuously exploring our interests, values, and strengths and making intentional choices that align with our purpose. By living a purposeful life, we can experience greater fulfillment and joy.

Chapter 9: The Interlude of Self-Reflection Self-reflection is the interlude that allows us to pause, reflect, and gain insights into our lives. It's the process of examining our thoughts, actions, and experiences to understand ourselves better. Self-reflection fosters personal growth, self-awareness, and mindfulness.

One way to practice self-reflection is through journaling. Writing about our experiences, thoughts, and emotions can provide clarity and perspective. It's a way to explore our inner world and gain insights into our behavior and motivations. Journaling can also help us process and release emotions, leading to greater emotional well-being.

Meditation is another powerful tool for self-reflection. It involves quieting the mind and focusing on the present moment. Meditation allows us to observe our thoughts without judgment and develop a deeper sense of self-awareness. Regular meditation practice can enhance our mindfulness and emotional regulation.

Seeking feedback from others can also contribute to self-reflection. Honest feedback from trusted friends, family, or mentors can provide valuable insights into our behavior and actions. It's about being open to constructive criticism and using it as an opportunity for growth. Feedback helps us identify areas for improvement and make positive changes.

Setting aside time for regular self-reflection is essential for personal growth. It's about creating moments of stillness and introspection in our busy lives. Self-reflection helps us gain clarity, make informed decisions, and align our actions with our values and goals.

By incorporating self-reflection into our daily routine, we can enhance our self-awareness, personal growth, and overall well-being. Self-reflection is a lifelong practice that allows us to continuously learn and evolve.

Chapter 10: The Choreography of Life Transitions Life transitions are the changing rhythms that mark different phases of our journey. They can be exciting and challenging, bringing new opportunities and uncertainties. Navigating life transitions requires resilience, adaptability, and a positive mindset.

One common life transition is the shift from education to career. Moving from the structured environment of school to the professional world can be daunting. It's about setting career goals, building skills, and seeking opportunities for growth. Networking and seeking mentorship can also provide guidance and support during this transition.

Another significant life transition is starting a family. Becoming a parent brings new responsibilities and joys. It's about balancing work and family life, creating a supportive home environment, and nurturing strong family bonds. Seeking support from family, friends, and community resources can help ease this transition.

Career changes are also common life transitions. Whether it's a promotion, a new job, or a career shift, these changes can be both exciting and stressful. It's about adapting to new roles, responsibilities, and work environments. Continuous learning, skill development, and seeking support from colleagues can help navigate career transitions successfully.

Life transitions also include personal changes such as relocation, retirement, or the loss of a loved one. These changes can bring a mix of emotions and challenges. It's about accepting and embracing change, seeking support, and finding ways to adapt and thrive. Resilience and a positive mindset are essential in navigating personal transitions.

Navigating life transitions requires self-compassion and patience. It's about being kind to ourselves and recognizing that change is a natural part of life. By approaching transitions with resilience and adaptability, we can embrace new opportunities and continue to grow and flourish.

Chapter 11: The Echo of Legacy Legacy is the echo that resonates beyond our lifetime, the impact we leave on the world and future generations. It's about making a positive difference and contributing to something greater than ourselves. Building a legacy involves aligning our actions with our values, passions, and goals.

One way to create a legacy is through acts of kindness and service. Small gestures of kindness can have a profound impact on others and create a ripple effect of positivity. Volunteering, supporting charitable causes, and helping those in need are ways to leave a lasting legacy of compassion and generosity.

Sharing our knowledge and skills is another way to build a legacy. Mentoring, teaching, and passing on our expertise can inspire and empower others. It's about investing in the growth and development of future generations. By sharing our wisdom, we can make a meaningful contribution to society.

Creating lasting memories with loved ones also contributes to our legacy. Spending quality time with family and friends, creating traditions, and celebrating milestones can create cherished memories. These memories serve as a reminder of the love and joy we shared and leave a lasting impact on our loved ones.

Documenting our stories and experiences is another way to preserve our legacy. Writing memoirs, recording videos, or creating photo albums can capture our journey and insights. It's about leaving behind a record of our life, values, and lessons learned. This documentation can serve as a source of inspiration and guidance for future generations.

Building a legacy is a lifelong journey that involves intentional actions and choices. It's about living with purpose, making a positive impact, and leaving behind a meaningful legacy that resonates beyond our time. By building a legacy, we can create a lasting influence and contribute to the betterment of the world.

Chapter 12: The Chorus of Gratitude Gratitude is the chorus that brings harmony and joy to our lives. It's the practice of recognizing and appreciating the positive aspects of our life. Cultivating gratitude enhances our well-being, relationships, and overall quality of life.

Practicing gratitude involves regularly reflecting on the things we are thankful for. It can be as simple as keeping a gratitude journal and writing down three things we are grateful for each day. This practice helps us focus on the positive aspects of our life and shift our perspective from scarcity to abundance.

Expressing gratitude to others is another powerful way to cultivate gratitude. Taking the time to thank and appreciate the people in our lives strengthens our relationships. It's about acknowledging the kindness, support, and contributions of others. Simple gestures such as writing thank-you notes or expressing appreciation in person can create a positive impact.

Mindfulness is also closely linked to gratitude. Being present and fully experiencing the moment allows us to appreciate the beauty and joy around us. Mindful practices such as meditation, deep breathing, and nature walks can enhance our sense of gratitude. It's about being aware of the small blessings and finding meaning and joy in everyday moments.

Practicing gratitude also involves shifting our mindset from scarcity to abundance. It's about recognizing that we have enough and appreciating what we have rather than focusing on what we lack. This shift in perspective can lead to greater contentment and happiness.

Gratitude is a powerful practice that can transform our lives. By cultivating gratitude, we can enhance our well-being, strengthen our relationships, and experience greater joy and fulfillment.

Chapter 13: The Coda of Compassion Compassion is the coda that brings a sense of unity and kindness to our lives. It's the ability to understand and alleviate the suffering of others. Practicing compassion enhances our empathy, strengthens our relationships, and contributes to a more compassionate world.

Self-compassion is the foundation of practicing compassion. It involves treating ourselves with kindness and understanding, especially during difficult times. Self-compassion allows us to acknowledge our imperfections and embrace our humanity. By being kind to ourselves, we can cultivate greater resilience and emotional well-being.

Practicing compassion towards others involves showing empathy, support, and understanding. It's about recognizing the struggles of others and offering a helping hand. Acts of compassion, whether big or small, can create a positive impact on those around us. It's about being present, listening, and offering support without judgment.

Compassion also extends to the broader community and world. Engaging in social and environmental causes, volunteering, and advocating for justice and equality are ways to practice compassion on a larger scale. It's about contributing to the greater good and making a positive difference in the world.

Cultivating a compassionate mindset involves developing greater empathy and understanding. Mindfulness practices, such as meditation and reflection, can help us cultivate compassion. It's about being aware of the interconnectedness of all beings and recognizing the impact of our actions.

Compassion is a powerful force that can transform our lives and the world around us. By practicing compassion towards ourselves and others, we can create a more compassionate and harmonious world.

Chapter 14: The Encore of Resilience Resilience is the encore that allows us to rise above challenges and continue our journey. It's the inner strength that enables us to bounce back from adversity and thrive in the face of difficulties. Developing resilience involves building a positive mindset, seeking support, and cultivating coping strategies.

One way to build resilience is by developing a growth mindset. A growth mindset is the belief that we can learn and grow from our experiences. It's about viewing challenges as opportunities for growth and embracing change. By cultivating a growth mindset, we can approach life with greater resilience and optimism.

Seeking support from others is another important aspect of resilience. Whether it's friends, family, or professional support, having a strong support system can help us navigate difficult times. It's about reaching out for help when needed and building connections that provide emotional and practical support.

Cultivating coping strategies is essential for building resilience. Coping strategies, such as mindfulness, exercise, and creative outlets, can help us manage stress and emotions. It's about finding healthy ways to process and release emotions, and developing a toolkit of coping mechanisms that work for us.

Building resilience also involves practicing self-care and prioritizing our well-being. Self-care activities, such as getting enough sleep, eating well, and engaging in activities we enjoy, can enhance our resilience. It's about taking care of ourselves physically, mentally, and emotionally.

Resilience is a lifelong journey that requires continuous effort and practice. By building resilience, we can navigate life's challenges with greater ease and continue to grow and flourish.

Chapter 15: The Finale of Flourishing Flourishing is the grand finale that brings together all the elements of a fulfilling life. It's the state of thriving, experiencing well-being, and living a life of purpose and meaning. Aligning health, wealth, and human connections is the key to flourishing.

Health provides the foundation for a flourishing life. By prioritizing our physical, mental, and emotional well-being, we can create a strong foundation for our overall quality of life. It's about making healthy choices, seeking support, and continuously working on our well-being.

Wealth, in its broader sense, provides the resources and opportunities to pursue our passions and goals. It's about achieving financial stability and making informed decisions that align with our values and aspirations. Building wealth allows us to access better opportunities and create a life of abundance.

Human connections bring meaning and joy to our lives. Strong relationships with family, friends, and community provide emotional support and a sense of belonging. It's about nurturing our relationships, practicing empathy, and creating meaningful connections.

Flourishing also involves finding purpose and aligning our actions with our values and passions. It's about setting meaningful goals, pursuing our interests, and making a positive impact on the world. By living a purposeful life, we can experience greater fulfillment and joy.

The journey to flourishing is an ongoing process that requires intentionality and effort. It's about continuously seeking balance, growth, and harmony in all aspects of our lives. By aligning health, wealth, and human connections, we can create a symphony of flourishing and lead a life of purpose and meaning.

A Symphony of Flourishing: Aligning Health, Wealth, and Human Connections

In "A Symphony of Flourishing," the interplay of health, wealth, and human connections is explored as a harmonious composition essential for a fulfilling life. This book delves into how these three pillars can be aligned to create a balanced and thriving existence.

Through fifteen engaging chapters, the book offers insights into achieving optimal physical and mental health, building financial stability, and nurturing meaningful relationships. Each chapter is crafted with elaborate paragraphs that provide practical advice, strategies, and personal reflections.

The narrative begins with the foundation of physical health, emphasizing the importance of nutrition, exercise, and preventive care. It then transitions to mental well-being, exploring stress management, resilience, and emotional intelligence. Financial stability is covered with discussions on budgeting, investing, and debt management, while the significance of strong human connections is highlighted through family, friendships, and community involvement.

As the book progresses, readers are guided through the nuances of work-life balance, finding purpose, and self-reflection. Life transitions and legacy-building are also addressed, offering a comprehensive view of leading a meaningful life. The concluding chapters emphasize gratitude, mindfulness, and the continuous journey of personal growth.

"A Symphony of Flourishing" is an inspiring guide for anyone seeking to harmonize the various aspects of life and achieve a state of flourishing. It encourages readers to embrace a holistic approach to well-being and offers practical tools for creating a balanced, joyful, and prosperous life.

www.ingramcontent.com/pod-product-compliance
Lightning Source LLC
LaVergne TN
LVHW020510080526
838202LV00057B/6271